Praise for *Brave Le.*

"This is a most unusual book. Fr. Juan Vélez presents the examined life, the life of the mind, as an adventure—full of thrills and daring and good humor. And that's what it is! Unfortunately, books for young people rarely convey this excitement. Brave Leader, Big Heart does it. Every Catholic young person should read this, but especially boys."

—Scott Hahn, author, professor of theology
at Franciscan University, Steubenville

"A fun and inspiring book about a fun and inspiring new saint. Fr. Juan's admiration for St. John Henry Newman shines through these pages. He brings the whole life of this hero of the faith to children in a relatable and accessible way, from Newman's creative, bookish childhood, through his courageous conversion, impressive scholarly achievement, and stalwart faithfulness."

—Kendra Tierney, author of Catholic All Year,
speaker, blogger, designer, and mother

"Bravery, Courage, and Perseverance—all qualities of St. John Henry Newman artfully depicted in *Brave Leader, Brave Heart*. This timely novel provides young readers inspiration and a roadmap to battle many of the same issues today which Newman faced two centuries ago."

—John Meyer, Executive Director, Napa Institute, which
strives to help leaders evangelize through their work

"I love the illustrations! The cover really captures the tone of the book and St. John Henry Newman's contemplative spirit. The letters and history tie the story together and make it very real, but also understandable for the young reader and invites him into an encounter with St. John Henry Newman where 'heart speaks to heart."

—Katie Bogner, Catholic School Teacher,
Director of Religious Education, blogger

"Brave Leader, Big Heart is an excellent introduction of St. John Henry Newman to junior high aged readers. The warmth of Fr. Juan Vélez's story-telling and the charming illustrations will draw students in and they will be sure to find a friend in St. John Henry. This book is a must for every middle school classroom."

—Bonnie Engstrom, author of *61 Minutes to a Miracle: Fulton Sheen and a True Story of the Impossible*, blogger, and mother

BRAVE LEADER,
BIG HEART

St. John Henry Newman's Adventures

BRAVE LEADER,
BIG HEART

St. John Henry Newman's Adventures

Juan Vélez

Scepter

Published by Scepter Publishers, Inc.
info@scepterpublishers.org
www.scepterpublishers.org
800-322-8773
New York

Cover design by Jennifer Calabretta, isimplydesign
Cover and interior illustrations by Manix Abrera, manixabrera.com
Text design and pagination by Carol Sawyer, Rose Design

Library of Congress Control Number: 2020940109

ISBN paperback: 9781594173875
ISBN eBook: 9781594173882

Printed in the United States of America

*To all the young people who read this book
and are inspired by the life of St. John Henry Newman.*

*And to Bruce and Barb Wyman (McNeese State University),
who are examples of Christian life for their students
as Newman was.*

Contents

1

Christian Heroes

The saints are Christian heroes. If God had sports teams, we could say that the saints are his best players and captains. They are leaders who exercise magnanimity, good judgment, courage, charity, and perseverance. John Henry was certainly all these: a great player and team captain. Just as captains lead their sports teams to victory, so do the saints of God. They are the captains we can follow to the best victory of all: heaven. There is something in a leader that commands attention, compelling others to follow. John Henry had this quality; his presence was such that others listened to what he said. Those around him realized that when he spoke or wrote, the words were sincere and came from his heart. They noticed that one of his most distinguishing characteristics was precisely this: his big heart. At the end of his long life, John Henry Newman chose for his motto: "Cor ad cor loquitur." This is a beautiful Latin phrase which means, "Heart speaks to heart." Newman knew that the hearts of saints were such that they could speak, but not with words. The hearts of saints speak to us through everyday actions and words, big and small. Some saints do great things from the seclusion of a convent cell, like St. Thérèse of Lisieux. But some saints do great things that the world can see more easily, and that's what John Henry Newman did.

At the same time, he was a normal boy, intelligent, fun-loving, and hard-working. He lived in a family with brothers, sisters, and parents who loved him very much. He began his life as many other English boys of his time. Let's continue on and let the heart of Newman speak to us.

John Henry was born and raised in England, part of a large island to the northwest of the European continent across the English Channel from France. England is the land of the Anglo-Saxons, inhabited originally by the ancient Celts who built mysterious stone structures like Stonehenge. At various other times England was inhabited by Romans, Saxons, Vikings, and Normans. This small island has produced great men and women of religious, literary, military, scientific, and political talent, people like King Alfred the Great, King Edward the Confessor, King Richard the Lion-Hearted, Geoffrey Chaucer, William Shakespeare, Charles Dickens, Queen Victoria, and Jane Austen. It numbers many saints too such as Augustine of Canterbury, Bede the Venerable, Thomas More, Edmund Campion, and Margaret Clitherow.

This is the story of the newest English saint: John Henry Newman.

We are lucky to know things about his early childhood because of letters both he and his parents wrote during that time. For example, from a letter his father wrote, we know that young John Henry was able to read well by the age of five. He was given adventure books to read and liked them very much.

2

Spy Club

John Henry grew up in a very exciting time in England. In the early 1800s, there were spies all over London, Paris, and other capitals of Europe: in the train stations, in the barber shops, in the stores, in the streets, in schools—everywhere. The American Revolution of 1776 was fresh on the minds of most people, and the English worried about a revolution in their own land.

In London at Ealing there was a well-known private boarding school run by Rev. David Nicholas. Lots of boys of different ages lived and studied there. One boy in particular was very smart and well-behaved; his name was John Henry Newman, and he was the head of the Spy Club. This club allowed the boys to think about the exciting world and the many things they heard being discussed all around them. They wanted to be heroes to help England. The boys talked about catching spies and going on dangerous missions, and they wrote stories for a school magazine called *The Spy*. But Newman secretly published a rival magazine, the *Anti-Spy*, which was alleged to be from an opposing faction. The Spy Club was a way for these boys to use their imagination, and John Henry had developed a good one. He had learned to imagine great things because he loved to read. Often times boys who read have minds filled with the stories and characters of their books and imagine the action that is happening right before them on the page. And this was true for him.

John Henry, a thin boy with big blue eyes, seemed to see and understand everything. He was quiet and calm except when he was in charge of the Spy Club. Then, his imagination came alive, and he would command authority. Everyone paid attention to him then because he could make his ideas seem to come alive. Already as a boy he had the qualities of a leader: conviction and the capacity of persuasion. This taught John Henry things that would help him later in life. He learned that the words he spoke could inspire those around him.

John Henry grew up in a loving family that supported him in his many interests. His father, originally from Cambridgeshire, was a banker in London. His mother descended from a strict Protestant family from northwestern France. He was born in London, the oldest of six children, three boys and three girls. The Newmans had a large summer house in Ham, on the outskirts of the city. It had a big chestnut tree in the back yard where John Henry liked to play and read about Aladdin and the Arabian Nights. At the age of five when Lord Nelson, a famous admiral, won the battle of Trafalgar the English lit candles inside of their windows to celebrate the victory. John Henry remembered the lighted windows glowing in the night. All these things excited his imagination, and he admired these brave men.

But there were many things to occupy the young boys John Henry's age that didn't have to do with battles or adventures. The boys at Ealing Grammar School liked acting in plays. John Henry was very good at memorizing lines and always participated. He also played the violin quite well. Learning the music and the rhythms of the measure of music helped train his ear. He understood what sounded pleasing and what did not sound pleasing. This sense of musical rhythm is an important part of education. It helps train the ear and the mind to recognize beauty. John Henry turned out to be a talented musician, and his love of rhythm remained with him all his life, helping him to write poetry and hymns. He enjoyed many composers, but his favorite was Ludwig van Beethoven, the famous German musician.

The boys in John Henry's school also learned Latin and Greek reading and composition. At that time, these languages were still part of a regular education. They studied Greek grammar and the Greek of the New Testament. They read in Greek from Homer's famous epics, *The Iliad* and *The Odyssey*. He loved the stories of the Greek heroes filled with adventure. In *The Iliad*, the valiant Hector fights to defend the city of Troy and his family but he is defeated by Achilles, the strongest Greek warrior. In *The Odyssey*, the Greek hero Odysseus (known as Ulysses in Roman myths), King of Ithaca, journeys home after the fall of Troy. Along the way he encounters all sorts of dangers and difficulties including the monster Cyclops, and the nymph Calypso who wishes to trap him on her island. After a ten year journey, Odysseus at last reaches his home and is only recognized at first by his faithful dog, Argus, who was a puppy when Odysseus left home. Argus had been waiting for Odysseus for 20 years. Odysseus soon reunites with his faithful wife, Penelope. After reading these exciting tales, John Henry dreamed of visiting Ithaca and other places where these Greek warriors had lived. But John Henry was also very good in Latin. He enjoyed Latin composition and at the age of ten he was already writing sentences. He loved the Latin language very much, and years later, when he was a priest, he would translate Latin hymns into English so that they could be more easily sung. Everything John Henry learned, he stored away in his treasure chest of knowledge. Sometimes, when a child is young, he might not understand why he has to learn this or that. But John Henry shows us that a good education is valuable for a whole life long.

All of these experiences together made such things as the Spy Club a natural activity for John Henry to begin. The Spy club was great fun, but what counted most were the tales of heroes, both ancient and modern. And then, one day, John Henry learned of some real-life heroes who lived in England. On Sunday, 18 June 1815, Lord Wellington, commanding the British forces, together with Field Marshal Blücher, at the head of the allied Prussian forces, defeated the dangerous tyrant Napoléon Bonaparte at Waterloo. This was an important battle! Europe was at last made safe. Young Newman was only a boy at the time, but he already had dreams of big and bold feats like the heroes he read about in his favorite books.

3

A Big Discovery

John Henry read many other types of books too,
not just books about heroes. Sometimes books
can be very helpful and teach valuable lessons,
but sometimes they can be confusing. This is what John
Henry learned, however the confusing things he read
taught him a very important lesson. This lesson was a

revelation and a new way of looking at the world. It was a big discovery. Usually when we think of discoveries, what comes to mind are events such as Magellan sailing around the world, the Wright Brothers' invention of the airplane, Edison's invention of the light bulb, or the Apollo 11 mission to the moon. But there are also discoveries that come about with words and ideas which have big consequences in people's lives and in the lives of others. When St. Augustine heard a voice in the garden saying *tolle et lege* (take and read) he was instructed by God to read a passage from St. Paul's letter to the Romans. This was a breakthrough that had to do with reading and ideas. Something similar happened to young Newman. It was less dramatic than what happened to St. Augustine, but like him it changed the course of John Henry's life. His change also had to do with a book. But before this he read some other literature that was questionable.

Since John Henry liked to read so much, he read whatever he got his hands on. When he was fifteen years old, he read some chapters of books that confused him because they contained errors about God and religion. One was written by David Hume, an English philosopher who did not believe that God could perform miracles. Another one was by Jacques Rousseau, a French philosopher with very dangerous ideas. It was a difficult time for the inquisitive young student, but one of the teachers at Ealing helped him to learn the truth.

The teacher was Mr. Mayers, a young graduate from Oxford University. He was a Christian of strong faith who inspired Newman. Mr. Mayers, realizing Newman's confusion, helped guide him towards good literature to read and thus resolved his doubts about God and religion.

One year, Newman became so ill that he couldn't go home from boarding school during his vacation. However, staying at school turned out to be a very good thing. He was able to talk more with the kind Mr. Mayers and one day young Newman made his big discovery! He realized that God, who is all-powerful, is within each one of us! John Henry understood that the mighty God who created the big ocean surrounding all of England, the mighty God who commanded the sun and the stars, this same mighty God was also present inside his soul, his very own soul! This realization was an encounter with God, and it changed John Henry forever.

He knew then that those books that had confused him were wrong. John Henry knew that not only did God exist, but God loved him! John Henry was excited because now he understood that he would never be alone again. All he had to do was close his eyes and realize that God was within him! Or he could open his eyes and see that only God could have made everything in nature around him: the thick woods, the lovely green hills, the deep blue sea, and the immense star-filled sky above him.

After this encounter with God, John Henry was sorry that the questionable writings had confused him. This regret that he felt deep within himself is known as the moral conscience and this conscience showed him in another way that God existed. God existed in this still small voice, helping him to choose rightly. He realized that he and everyone else needed to think always about God before doing things that might displease Him. Because John Henry realized that God cared very much about him, he did not wish to offend God. God was no longer just a powerful being, but a loving father who cared about him! Not only that, God wanted to know each person as a dear friend. This realization made the young teenager very happy. He felt filled with delight by this amazing truth . . . that God loved him, and that he would never ever be without this Friend. His heart was now filled with God, but much more than just the idea of God; it was a personal relationship with God.

John Henry had figured out something very fundamental . . . that Christianity is much more than rules and regulations, Christianity is about being God's children. The rules and regulations were for a purpose, and that was to help persons to live as good sons and daughters of God. From that time on, Newman's life was never the same. God was real and personal: a Father and a Great Friend. John Henry knew that his life mattered to God. And this great understanding would set the course for the rest of Newman's life. He became a Christian soldier, not on a battlefield, but in many other ways: He wouldn't be using a rifle or a sword on this battlefield, but pen and ink. He would have to be very brave, and he would face many obstacles and even some enemies. John Henry used these "weapons" courageously to do incredible good.

Throughout these times of growing and learning, John Henry was fun-loving and friendly. He wrote happy and humorous letters to his sisters which give a little glimpse into his personality. In one letter he wrote in reply to his sister Jemima, he said, "One thing in your letter disappointed me very much, and this it was. At the end you say, we all send our love with your affectionate sister, J.C. Newman. I consequently very naturally supposed that you were sent to me, as your letter seems to imply it, and as there was a lumbering heavy *lump* of *something* or other at the bottom of the parcel, I concluded it must be you, and so I began to unpack this rapidly, to give you (as I thought) some fresh air, of which I did not doubt that you were in want. When to my surprise, having unpacked the said heavy lump, it proved to be cake! . . . Believe me ever, my dear Jemima, your affectionate Brother."

Time passed, and John Henry was growing up; it was time to move to his next school.

Growing in Valor at
Trinity College

Trinity College! Trinity College is a famous school with a big name at Oxford, the oldest and most important university in England. Oxford

University, established in the eleventh century, and Cambridge, established in the thirteenth century, both universities founded by Catholics, had become Anglican in the sixteenth century after the Protestant Reformation. Each was made up of many colleges, and each college had its own buildings including a chapel, a staff consisting of a head of the college, teachers called tutors, and students. John Henry's father took his son to Trinity College, and John Henry was accepted at the age of 15. The young man was eager to start at Trinity, but he needed to wait one more year.

Going to college is a big step in a young person's life. There are so many new things to learn and new people to meet. Even though he was excited when he began college the next year, he still met with some challenges. It was especially difficult for Newman, despite being very capable, because he was young and somewhat shy. Newman wasn't sure how to fit in with the other young men. This is often the case when a young person leaves home for the first time. It's very difficult to know just what to do! The young men at Trinity college were carefree and hadn't yet learned to think much about religious ideas and other things that interested John Henry. The difference between the quiet, thinking Newman, and the boisterous young men was very great. Newman had already conceived of big goals and he seemed more serious than his classmates; but even so, he was very happy. And his new understanding of friendship with God was still very fresh in his mind, setting him apart from some of his classmates. But the situation was about to get easier for him. The first week at Trinity, John Henry met William Bowden who was a few years older than he. William Bowden was another thoughtful and responsible young man. Their similarities made them become friends right away, and soon Newman began to spend vacations at his friend's home on the Isle of Wight, a lovely island on the southern coast of England.

For two years in a row he travelled with his friend William to the beautiful Isle of Wight and in later years he thought fondly of these visits. Later he traveled to the home of another friend, Richard Hurrell Froude, in Dartington, close to the southern coast of England. Newman described the enchanting countryside of Dartington in this way: "What strikes me most is the strange richness of everything. The rocks blush into every variety of color, the trees and fields are emeralds, and the cottages are rubies." The purple and orange color of the sunset in the nearby Dartmoor Heights was so striking that he thought the Isle of Wight by contrast seemed drawn in pencil. These two early friends, Bowden and Froude, became very important to John Henry and their friendships also bore rich fruit. Bowden, like Newman, liked to write and together the two wrote a play on the St. Bartholomew's Day Massacre.

Having Bowden as a friend at Trinity was a big help. But there were other things happening at school that bothered Newman. One of these things was that many of the students drank a lot of alcohol.

"Have another pint! We can drink all we want . . . Go on—take another one!" Many young students drank too much and ended up drunk. They felt like no one was watching since they were away from their parents. They did not know how to use their freedom well. Some of the men tried to get Newman to play the violin and drink with them. Some tried to bully Newman, to shame him into doing things he felt uncomfortable doing, but he held on to his beliefs and just said no. That still small voice of his inner conscience reminded him that he did not want to disappoint God, his Creator, Savior, and greatest friend. It takes bravery to say "no" to popular things that are happening all around. But John Henry did, and as such he became a good example to the boys.

Another situation that upset Newman was that few of the men seemed to be interested in religion, and they lacked reverence for God. After a night of heavy drinking, they would attend the communion service of the Anglican church. They mostly went to the service not because they wanted to, but because it was a rule of the college. Newman could not accept this irreverent behavior. Since he had learned to love Jesus, he knew these actions would make Jesus very sad. Plus, he remembered that St. Paul taught that we should not receive the Lord unworthily in communion.

Despite all these difficult social situations, Trinity College was still a good place to study for students who were eager to learn and Newman was one of these interested students. He worked hard. His tutor, Dr. Short, guided him in the reading required for final exams. He continued to read classical Greek authors: the philosopher Aristotle, the mathematician Euclid, the historian Thucydides, the playwrights Aeschylus and Euripides, as well as some Latin authors. When Dr. Short thought he was ready for the college exams, he urged Newman to take them. But the young student got very nervous during the finals. He passed the exams but did not get a high score. He felt discouraged and embarrassed by his failure to do so. However, he did not quit.

At this point in his education, his father offered him some advice. "I would like you to study law and become a lawyer," Mr. Newman told his son. For some time, John Henry listened to his father and enrolled in law classes in London at Lincoln Inn. Although he wanted to please his father, he was not content studying law, and instead his interests in religion and religious practices continued to grow. The Holy Spirit was working inside John Henry helping him discern his path in life. After a year of law studies, he returned to Trinity College. One day in 1822, John Henry's father, who loved his son very much and was concerned about how he would make a living, told him "make up your mind what you are going to do!" He wanted his son to fulfil his potential and use his talents. Newman chose the religious life, and thereafter, found his focus: to study at Oxford so that he could receive the sacrament of Holy Orders. But as serious as he was about his studies, Newman did not neglect other aspects of life.

Even with all his studies and preparing for exams, Newman found time for rest. He enjoyed riding horses with friends. It was good physical exercise and a time for great conversations. The cool air and beautiful country scenes were refreshing. He also pursued other hobbies and continued to practice playing the violin. By this time, he was quite a good musician and could play in ensembles with others.

With all the new experiences Newman encountered at Trinity, he was lucky because he had found many good teachers. Good teachers make a great difference. Through all his study, as well as the hardships and challenges that he met, Newman was learning about himself and becoming more self-assured. He was coming into his own and growing up—developing talents for writing and speaking. He had developed his capacity for conversation and friendship. He had become a well-rounded person who not only concentrated on his studies, but also his music, outdoor activities, his friendships, and most importantly, his special friendship with Jesus.

Newman considered this period of his life as a very happy time. He once wrote that he wanted to be like the simple snapdragon flower which grew on the walls of Trinity College and which he passed daily. There were two reasons for this. First, Newman, like the snapdragon, wanted to remain and teach at the university all of his life. So, he decided that he would prepare for a competition which would allow him to stay at Oxford and teach at Oriel College. The second lesson he learned from considering the snapdragon was that it was a humble plant; happy to bloom right where it was, even though it was growing on a stone wall instead of in a beautiful field. This struck Newman especially because with all his successes, he had become very proud. Being proud of a job well done is a good thing, but being overly proud because of the enjoyment of being praised is called hubris, the wrong kind of pride. This insight was so vivid to him that he prayed for humility and later wrote a poem about this named "The Snapdragon."

5

Reforming Oriel College

Trinity was only one of the colleges at Oxford. Oriel, the fifth oldest college at Oxford, was another. Colleges are divisions within a university. Modern universities still have separate colleges much like in Newman's day, that often focus on a separate area of academics. Oriel was founded in 1324, before the Protestant Reformation, and its original name was the College of the Blessed Virgin Mary. In the courtyard, above an arch, was a small statue of the Virgin Mary, a detail that caught Newman's eye. However, a few years after being established, the college received a large house by the name of La Oriole, and this is how it acquired the common name of "Oriel."

During Newman's time at Oxford, Oriel College was known for being advanced in its approach to teaching students. One way that Oriel was advanced was that it opened its academic competition to graduates from other colleges. These competitions were for students to become fellows, a special category of students, who became members of a college for life. Newman entered the competition, did well on the examination, and was chosen for this honor. Becoming a fellow of Oriel was a big accomplishment, and he immediately wrote to tell his parents the good news.

Oriel had many good teachers who helped shape John Henry. These teachers taught him to think and encourage him to write, but more importantly, they helped John Henry learn how to think about others besides himself. They helped him understand how to live the Golden Rule to grow in his understanding of the Christian faith. Some of them also taught Newman not only by the words that they spoke and lessons that they taught, but by their personal witnesses. That is, they were good role models, showing that they believed what they taught, and these witnesses impacted Newman very much. One in particular, a poetry teacher named John Keble, had written a book of Christian poetry called *The Christian Year*. It greatly influenced Newman, who had always loved to write verses and he saw that verses, or poetry, could be an effective and pleasing way to communicate.

In 1824, Newman moved to the next step in his religious life and was ordained a deacon in the Anglican church. He was assigned as an assistant at the small parish of St. Clement. The following year he was ordained an Anglican priest. Filled with emotion he wrote: "What a divine service is that of ordination!" He continued at St. Clement's and made it a point to visit families and sick persons. He was so good and kind that one day when he visited a sick elderly woman, she felt that Jesus himself had come to visit her. Many people felt this same warmth when in John Henry Newman's presence. The Holy Spirit had quietly continued his work within Newman's soul and had given him the gift of kindness.

Even with his church duties, Newman was soon appointed a tutor, or teacher, at Oriel College. Tutors were college fellows whose job it was to help students with their studies. Newman, along with two of his friends, William Wilberforce and Richard Hurrell Froude, thought that a tutor should do more than just help students learn their school lessons. They believed a tutor should be concerned with the whole student, especially the student's moral and religious life. They knew from their own experiences that life is much more than just excelling in school. Life is about pleasing God.

In order to help shape the whole student, Newman, the young tutor, would go on long walks or horseback rides with his students, remembering how much these personal encounters had helped him when he was growing up. During summer vacations he would offer them extra classes to help them prepare for exams. He treated them as friends rather than just students. He was concerned for their religious practices and how they lived their lives outside of the classroom. This method worked well. Frederick Rogers, one of Newman's best students, later became a successful man. And the Mozley brothers, also Newman's students, later married his sisters, Harriet and Jemima.

But not everyone thought these changes were good. The head of Oriel College, a man named Hawkins, at first allowed these new ways of helping the students, but later he changed his mind. Newman knew that the way he and others had begun to form students was right, but Hawkins would not give in. And so, Hawkins quit assigning students to Newman. This was a big blow to John Henry because his plan had failed. But these ideas would live inside Newman, and he would apply them at other schools. Years later, one of his most famous books called *The Idea of a University* would contain some of his ideas. Newman had other big plans for reform too. And these plans would impact his life. But before the next chapter of his life began, Newman took an exciting trip with an unexpected outcome.

6

Newman's Mediterranean Trip

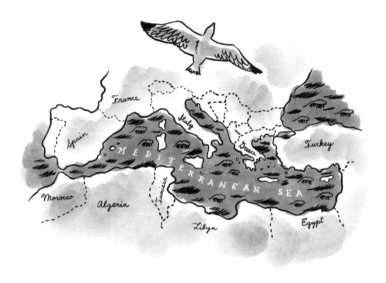

Young people, with their bold and curious minds, often dream of exploring far off lands and making new discoveries. Some of them actually follow their dreams and become famous. For example, in 1271, at the age of 17, Marco Polo traveled with his father and uncle across the Mediterranean Sea to the Holy Land, and from there through Armenia and Persia to China to visit the great Kublai Khan. The

Mediterranean Sea is also filled with all sorts of islands, big and small and for countless years, they have been stopping places for many explorers.

The Mediterranean Sea was dotted with colonies along its borders. Sailors from many lands like ancient Phoenicia, Greece, and Rome sailed the Mediterranean Sea, along with fearsome pirates. It was also the sea of the *Iliad* and the *Odyssey*. In biblical times, St. Paul sailed across the Mediterranean Sea to stand trial in Rome. Crusaders had crossed the Mediterranean back and forth on their mission to free the Holy Land, and later Napoleon Bonaparte crossed it in order to conquer empires in Egypt. For centuries navies had crossed the Mediterranean to gain and protect empires, or transport wheat from Egypt to the harbors of the Roman empire.

John Henry knew about all of the exploits of past explorers and conquerors, of the lands and seas they had traveled and the things they had done, from the books he had read when younger. His vivid imagination allowed him to wonder about all the different places that had been described in those stories. When he was a young boy, he had hoped one day to see them and his dreams were soon to come true. It could not have happened at a better time. After he was no longer able to teach at Oriel College, Newman left his position as tutor. He was, of course, very sad about his decision, though he knew it was right. But at this very moment came a chance of a lifetime: to sail the Mediterranean

Sea! He was given the opportunity to accompany his good friend, Richard Hurrell Froude. Froude suffered from a dangerous lung disease called tuberculosis. His doctor suggested that the warmer climates of the Mediterranean Sea might be good for Hurrell because England can be very cold and rainy.

Even though it was common in Newman's time for wealthy students to travel and make a "grand tour of Europe," Newman realized that an occasion such as this might not come by again. So, he gladly set out with Froude and his father on a small steamer from Falmouth, England. After they rounded the coast of Portugal, they stopped to visit Gibraltar. There they visited powerful fortifications and saw many beautiful views and gardens. They continued to the island of Malta and then to the western islands off Greece: Zante, Corfu, and then Ithaca, the island of Odysseus!

The sights of Ithaca and of Greece brought to memory, not only Odysseus, but all the Greek heroes he had loved reading about as a child. He experienced many more happy memories when, during the trip home, he visited the remains of Greek amphitheaters near Naples and Sicily. After visiting one particular ancient temple on a hilltop in Greece he wrote to his sister, ". . . Oh that I could tell you one quarter of what I have to say about it—but neither memory nor expression serve me! Wonderful place, piercing the heart with a strange painful pleasure." The reason this gave Newman pain is because the beautiful temple wasn't a church built for Christ, but for the false pagan gods of old.

Every day aboard the steamer, Newman wrote long letters to family and friends; he liked to tell stories and he was very good at it. He also enjoyed writing short verses, or poems. These verses were religious and about Newman's love for Christ and the Church. Before setting out on the voyage, Newman had promised to write some short poems to a friend, Hugh Rose, who was a journal editor. The men thought that Newman's religious verses might help people love the Church more. Newman and his friends wished to invigorate the spirit of the Anglican church, to encourage people to love Christ through the church.

But a frightening thing also happened on this long journey. On the island of Sicily, Newman became very sick from a potentially life-threatening infection. This was the time before modern drugs, like antibiotics. Nevertheless, even though he was dangerously ill, he told his servant and a doctor who cared for him that he was sure he would not die. "I think God has work for me yet," he calmly told them. He believed God had given him a mission to accomplish back home in England. The young Newman now realized that God expected him to work for the renewal of the Church. But Newman was sick for many weeks and couldn't yet travel. Despite missing home, he was filled with hope because he knew God had a plan for him. This time of illness and quiet thinking about God had a very profound impact on Newman and this remained with him throughout his life. When he was finally well enough to return home, he boarded a ship from Palermo to Marseilles, traveled by land across France, crossed the English Channel, and at long last, returned to England.

During his homeward voyage, he wrote his famous poem, "Lead Kindly Light." He asked God to be his light, to show him the work that he should do for Him. He was satisfied if he could but see the path one step at a time: "Keep thou my feet; I do not ask to see/ The distant scene—one step enough for me." This well-known poem is now sung as a hymn at many churches. Like Marco Polo and other explorers who had sailed the Mediterranean, he had another long journey ahead of him. But this new journey would not take him to more distant lands; it was the beginning of a journey that one day would take him away from the Anglican church. That would not happen for many more years, and he needed faith in God and perseverance.

7

Reviving the Anglican Church

After his influential voyage and illness, and with his new understanding of God's mission for him, John Henry began to act. He was going to do his best to help renew the Anglican church. He did this by what he wrote and what he said. He was a young clergyman and full of energy. "CHOOSE YOUR SIDE. To remain neutral much longer will be itself to take a part," Newman courageously told the other English clergy. He and his friends realized that the Anglican Church had lost its power and independence; it needed reform. How had this happened? It was all because of a headstrong, former King of England.

In the 1530s, England was still a Catholic country, and the king, Henry VIII, wanted to break one of the laws of the Catholic Church. To do this, he had to seize power, so he declared himself the Supreme Head of the Church in England in order to separate the English Church from the authority of the Pope. Henry VIII wanted to divorce his wife to marry someone else. The Pope would not grant him an annulment for his marriage, and this made the king angry. He didn't like being told no. So, he decided that he would take matters into his own hands and say that the Pope was wrong. He started a new church and called it the Church of England. This was the beginning of the Anglican Church. As a result, the Catholic bishops in England lost control of the Church. Henry VIII didn't want anything to stand in his way, and so all the priests and bishops had a decision to make. Did they give their faith to the true Catholic Church, or did they bow to King Henry and his new church? Henry VIII was brutal. If someone said they would not obey his new church, the king would put them in prison or kill them. And so slowly over the years, after the death of many brave priests and citizens such as St. John Fisher and St. Thomas More, the Anglican Church replaced the Catholic Church and became the only Church in England. By the time John Henry was born almost 300 years later, the former Catholic churches and cathedrals were now Anglican.

As a result of King Henry removing the Pope's power in order to have his way, many other constant teachings soon changed as well. All the teachings of the Catholic Church in England were watered down to please those in power. Since the bishops were subject to the King rather than to the Pope (and therefore to Christ) this meant that many teachings became even weaker over time. Without the Pope and without the teaching authority of the Catholic Church, the King or the government became the head of the Anglican Church. This was the predicament of the Church of England at the time of John Henry Newman.

And this is why "choose your side" was the challenge that Newman laid out to clergymen throughout England. He wanted the beliefs and practices which had been watered down to become stronger, because he loved the Anglican Church. The Catholic Church had all but disappeared by this time. Newman and some of his friends at Oxford began to write pamphlets defending the Anglican Church's self-rule, true beliefs, and traditional practices. They realized the danger of having the government in control of church matters and wanted to warn others about it because there had already been much loss of faith in England. The attempt by Newman and his friends to reform and strengthen the Anglican Church was named the Oxford Movement. This movement had an effect throughout all of England. And Newman was its principal leader.

Besides writing pamphlets, commonly called tracts, Newman delivered sermons every Sunday at his parish, St. Mary the Virgin, the most important church at Oxford. His powerful sermons urged students and professors to a personal renewal of faith. Newman told them that God was calling them to live holy Christian lives; God wanted them to worship him and obey his commandments and precepts. These teachings were not new, but Newman was a master teacher. He explained things clearly and strongly using many bible passages. He understood the hearts of many people. Whoever heard Newman was struck by his sermons and remembered them. Even today people read his sermons and learn from them. Writing had become Newman's weapon in the battle for the souls of men. And as is the case in all battles, the warriors need to be courageous, something John Henry would soon learn first-hand.

Thanks to all this hard work, many Anglican clergy and laity joined the Oxford Movement, and it continued to spread. Many others were convinced of the need to reform the Anglican Church too, but then something else happened. Soon people began to worry that being in the Oxford Movement would lead to becoming Roman

Catholic. At this time in history, most people didn't understand the Catholic Church because the Anglican Church had been in power for so long. Newman had no intention of leading people to the Catholic Church; he was trying to make the Anglican Church better. However many people, including bishops, did not agree with the ideals of the Oxford Movement.

One example of a disagreement between John Henry and another clergyman happened over something that should be a happy occasion, a wedding. Marriage was a sacrament in the Anglican Church, and it was to be done following church teachings, or doctrines, which were Christian. Many persons did not give any importance to these doctrines because of the problems John Henry had identified; they looked at the sacraments as simple social ceremonies instead of sacred rites that produce the grace for which they are signs. One day a man came to ask Newman to perform his daughter's marriage. When Newman asked the father, "Has she been baptized?" the father replied, "No." Newman, the fearless young priest, in turn replied, "I cannot marry her; she must first be baptized." And so the wedding was performed by another clergyman in the city. The newspapers mocked Newman, and the bishop, instead of backing Newman who was in the right, agreed with the father of the unbaptized woman that Newman should perform the marriage. Imagine how much this hurt Newman, who knew he was following God's law. But more battles were to come.

Another showdown happened when Newman published *Tract 90*, a booklet which is now very famous. In this writing, Newman proposed that most of the principles of the Anglican Church (known as the Thirty-Nine Articles) could have a Catholic interpretation. The Thirty-Nine articles are statements of faith that Anglicans are supposed to believe and are found in Anglican prayer books still to this day. What Newman was trying to say in *Tract 90* is that Anglican and Catholic beliefs were compatible. *Tract 90* was discussed by many and condemned repeatedly by one bishop after another. It was being discussed and argued about. Newman felt that he could not take back what he had written, but in good conscience, he could not continue to teach undergraduates at St. Mary's since his beliefs were met with such opposition. He made another brave decision; he decided to move away from his beloved and safe position as rector of St. Mary's parish to take up residence at the mission church of Littlemore. "My preaching days in our church are over," Newman wrote a friend. He wanted to read, think, and pray about what he should do next. He bought some stables and turned them into simple lodgings for himself and some friends who decided to follow him there. There they lived a simple and strict schedule of prayer and study. This way of living looked to some people like the life of Catholic monks, but

Newman and his young friends did not wear habits or take monastic vows. Still, some visitors accused Newman to the bishop of having a monastery or of being a secret Catholic. People were astounded that the very successful and prominent John Henry Newman would leave his prestigious life to live in a rural area in an old cow barn. It was a courageous thing to do.

For the next five years he studied and prayed at Littlemore. Many people visited to spend time with Newman and to seek his guidance. Littlemore was to be a place of great awakening for Newman, who was trying very hard to follow God's will for him.

8

The Decision to Become Roman Catholic

n the many letters that he wrote during all these years, Newman told his sisters and closest friends what was going through his mind. In one letter to a friend he wrote, "I cannot make out why I am to believe just what the English Church allows me to believe and nothing more." Newman's heart had been filled with the desire to please God ever since his "discovery" as a boy. With this big heart, he continued to pursue religious truth passionately. He was ready to give up his respected position at Oxford, or even to suffer for his beliefs, in order to follow what his conscience told him was true. He greatly loved the Anglican Church, even with its faults, and he wanted to remain Anglican while he worked to help the church he loved. But in praying and studying at Littlemore, including reading the Fathers of the Catholic Church, little by little he was becoming Roman Catholic. The Holy Spirit was working in Newman.

To become Roman Catholic in Newman's time required bravery. People were suspicious of Catholics and their religious practices. Some people even accused him of being a Jesuit spy who was only pretending to be an Anglican. Three hundred years earlier, right after the turmoil caused by Henry VIII, English Jesuit priests had been imprisoned or killed for offering the sacrifice of the Mass. Queen Elizabeth, who ruled soon after Henry VIII, had St. Edmund Campion, a brilliant scholar and Oxford graduate, tortured and killed for the "crime" of offering the Catholic sacraments to the faithful. This happened to many others as well. By Newman's time, the situation was not as dangerous for Catholics, but they were still treated with disdain and ridicule.

Newman, the bright Oxford teacher, gradually began to question whether the Anglican Church was a valid church. One of the main reasons for his doubts was the control the Anglican Church still allowed the British government to have over the church. "A Church that is ruled by the civil government cannot be the fold of Christ," he thought. Jesus had said: "Give to Caesar what is Caesar's and to God what is God's." The Church that Jesus founded exists in a civil society, but it should not follow orders from a king or president. The Church must respect civil government, but also, civil government should respect the Church.

Despite his conflicting thoughts regarding the Anglican Church, Newman considered matters carefully. Often, young men who were thinking of becoming Catholic would come to him for advice. Newman wisely told them to be patient and wait; they should not act with haste. Becoming Catholic is a life-changing event, and something so important should be accompanied by prayer, discernment, and guidance. Newman was an excellent guide for those who sought his advice.

While at Littlemore, he began writing down notes for a book that would help him come to a decision on whether or not to believe the Catholic Church. For some time, he had thought that certain Catholic beliefs about papal authority, the Mass, purgatory, and prayers to the saints, especially teachings regarding the Virgin Mary, were errors or exaggerations. These are some of the things that still confuse Protestants today. Newman studied history to see how these Catholic beliefs and practices developed in the ancient church. He also wished to examine if these beliefs were good or bad developments after the death of Christ, while the Church through the ages was forming its doctrines.

Time passed, and by 1844, through much study and prayer, Newman drew closer to accepting the teachings of the Catholic Church. His friends, John Keble and Edward Pusey, tried to talk him out of his new conviction. They could not understand why their good friend and, up to then, the leader of the Oxford Movement, had begun to think this way. Unfortunately, their disagreement sadly caused them to part ways. Other friends, Edward Manning and Edward Gladstone, later a Prime Minister, also tried to prevent Newman from continuing on the path towards the Catholic faith. Gladstone wrote to his friends that losing Newman to Catholicism would be the greatest loss since the start of the Protestant Reformation in the sixteenth century.

By the fall of 1845, some of Newman's close friends, one by one, began to convert to the Catholic Church. At long last came his turn. His conscience told him that to save his soul he must become Roman Catholic. He had received so many lights from God about the Church that he knew in his heart that if he were to die without becoming Catholic, God would hold him accountable for this failure to do so. This step to become Catholic took wisdom and courage. It meant leaving behind some friends and even family members, but with the light of the Holy Spirit, John Henry Newman understood that this was the path to take.

Yet another huge life-changing event happened quietly on October 9th, 1845. The previous day Newman instructed a friend to ask an Italian missionary, Fr. Dominic Barberi, a Passionist priest traveling in England, to stop by Littlemore. The priest arrived on the eve of the 8th, drenched in rain after traveling several hours on the upper deck of a stagecoach. Fr. Dominic, wet and cold, was standing before a fire drying his clothes when Newman entered the room. He could hardly believe his eyes! There was John Henry Newman, the famous and influential Oxford clergyman, humbly coming to him to make a general confession. On the morning of the 9th, Newman made his profession of faith and received the Holy Eucharist. He was now a Roman Catholic. This was a conversion that would rock the Protestant world in England. With this decision, Newman acted as a courageous spiritual leader who showed the way for others, especially Protestants, to consider the Catholic faith.

Newman later beautifully wrote that his conversion to the Catholic Church was like a ship coming to port after a stormy sea. He felt peace in his soul and he never again doubted the truth about Catholicism. But he did not look down on his former Anglican friends and co-religionists. He had simply followed the path the Holy Spirit had laid out for him and taken steps that, little by little, led him to the Church of Rome. He had finally come to understand that this was the Church of great fourth century saints and teachers like St. Athanasius and St. Basil. He had read their works, and at one point had even thought, "If St. Athanasius and St. Basil were to wake up from the dead, which Church would they recognize as their own?" The answer was clear: The Roman Catholic Church. John Henry Newman to this day leads others by his sincere witness and passion for truth. Littlemore now held very special significance for Newman, and it still exists today. It has been preserved for people to come and visit where John Henry Newman became Catholic.

9

From Oxford
to the City of Rome

John Henry Newman was now a Roman Catholic. But he had more life-altering decisions to make, difficult decisions. Leaving a place where you have lived for many years can be very difficult, even more so if this place has meant a lot to you. This was exactly the case with Newman's change from Anglicanism to Catholicism. Anglicanism had been home for so much of his life; he had loved and worked tirelessly for the Anglican Church, and now he had left this home. He spent the last night at Littlemore all by himself, and though he felt alone, he felt very close to God. The next day Newman said good-bye to his friends, among them his old college tutor, an astronomer friend, and Edward Pusey, and also to his beloved Oxford where he had lived almost thirty years.

He moved for a short time to Oscott College, renamed Maryvale (the land of Mary), in a town north of Oxford. From Oscott he traveled to Rome with another convert, Ambrose St. John. He and Ambrose St. John were destined to become best friends. They went to Rome following the advice of Bishop Wiseman to study for the Catholic priesthood. The two converts lived at the College of Propaganda Fide with youths who went there to study and become future priests for mission countries.

Only a few weeks after their arrival in Rome, John Henry and Ambrose were called by surprise to see Pope Pius IX. The Pope struck Newman as a healthy middle-aged man with a kind look and manner. The Pope spoke to them about the conversion of an English clergyman—referring to Newman. When Ambrose St. John innocently asked, "What is his name?" the Italian Pope good-humoredly placed his hand on Ambrose's arm and said: "Do you think I can pronounce your English names?"

And so began Newman's time of study in Rome. He was well-received at the College of Propaganda Fide but was disappointed by the academic level. He thought it should be more difficult. And when he wished to study St. Thomas Aquinas, he was told that this great theologian was not then popular in Rome. Luckily, one of the most respected teachers in Rome, Fr. Giovanni Perrone, treated him well; together, Fr. Perrone and Newman read and discussed many things, including the book that Newman had finished writing before his conversion.

Eagerly, Newman continued his studies for the priesthood with a few other convert friends who had also come with him from Littlemore. Newman thought about what to do once they were all ordained priests. He could think of three possibilities: They could either join the Jesuits, the Benedictines, or the Congregation of the Oratory of St. Philip Neri. Newman was attracted by all three but after discernment, which is a period of thought and prayer, he decided that he preferred the Oratory. He had been attracted to the Oratory because of its sixteenth century founder, St. Philip Neri. St. Philip had a great personality; he was humble and magnanimous. He was a charitable man and wise counselor to rich and poor, with a wonderful sense of humor. He was happy and liked to laugh. Newman also liked the flexibility the Oratory gave to priests. It allowed them to carry out different ministries based on their specific talents.

Once his friends agreed to join the Oratory with him, they asked the Pope for his approval, which he quickly granted. "We are to be Oratorians. The Pope has been very kind to us," he wrote a friend. They were ordained priests in Rome on May 30, 1847. After so many years of prayer, study, and heartache, Newman was able to say Mass for the first time. His difficult journey had brought him to this amazing privilege, to be a Roman Catholic priest.

During this period, before returning to England, he wrote the novel *Loss and Gain* which is partially based on his own experiences. In it, the main character, an Oxford student who converts to Catholicism, enters a church while the Sacrifice of the Mass is being offered. The student is struck by the beauty and the reverence of the Mass. This novel helps show what Newman was thinking about at this important time of his life.

Then, one day, Pope Pius IX asked Newman to perform a big task. He asked Newman to take the Oratory of St. Philip to England. Newman agreed and he became the founder of the first English Oratory, which exists to this day. He and his companions established it in Birmingham, an industrial city filled with many poor Irish immigrants who had moved there to work. Today people can visit the Oratory's museum where they can see many personal items that belonged to St. John Henry Newman, the most famous convert in England.

10

Helping Irish Immigrants in Birmingham

There was much work for the new Roman Catholic priest to do. Fr. Newman arrived in Birmingham during a tragic period of history for England's neighboring country, Ireland. From

1845–1849, an infection spread from field to field, killing off most of the potato crops. This time is known as the Great Potato Famine. The lack of potatoes, plus politics involving the British government and money, made the famine devastating for the Irish people. Families were starving. About one million people died and another million left Ireland for other countries, including the United States. However, there was a very large immigration to Birmingham because of its nearness to Ireland and the availability of work for the starving immigrants. Even people without skills could find jobs in Birmingham's many factories and shops. Ireland was a Catholic country so most of the immigrants were Catholic. They faced serious problems in their new country: avoiding crime, finding housing, and obtaining health care. They also needed care for their souls.

Fr. Newman and his group of new priests had their work cut out for them. They were moved by charity to begin work that would help the immigrants. They bought a former gin factory, remodeled it for their own first home and included a chapel. At the chapel's opening, five to six hundred people came. The Catholic immigrants now, at least, had care for their souls. The priests provided religious instruction and the sacraments. Newman heard many confessions for these poor men, women, and children.

Before becoming Catholic, Newman had not understood much of the political fighting and social activism of those who were interested in the welfare of the Irish. The Irish activists wanted Ireland to be freed from English rule and improve their living conditions. Now that Fr. Newman was working alongside them in Birmingham, he saw firsthand their unjust and miserable living and working conditions. He also understood better why the English bishops had sided with the activists who wanted to help their situation.

In the following years, although Newman would also open a boarding school in Birmingham for students of well-to-do families, nevertheless for most of his life he remained in Birmingham serving the poor. He did have to leave Birmingham for a time, however, but this was for an important project with lasting consequences. He was asked to start a Catholic university in Dublin, which became the first Catholic University in all of Ireland.

11

The First Catholic University in Ireland

t takes a big heart and mind to think about such things as starting a university. John Henry was just such a person. He possessed the virtue called "magnanimity." Magnanimity means greatness of soul, from the Latin for *magna* (great) and *anima* (soul). Good Leaders have greatness of soul. They think big, with a noble ambition. And they think about the good of society more than their own personal needs. Magnanimous people have a vision to help others. They are also able to convey this vision to others and get them to follow. Since Newman possessed this virtue, he was ready for the challenge to help start the first Catholic university in Ireland.

So how did it come about that Fr. Newman was asked to leave his important work in Birmingham to embark on this new mission? It happened this way. One day in 1851, Paul Cullen, Archbishop of Dublin, visited Birmingham. Archbishop Cullen knew about the famous John Henry Newman, and he realized that it would take someone like Fr. Newman to tackle such a task as starting a university. 'We need your name, AND we need your knowledge,' said the archbishop to the surprised Newman. Although the request caught him off guard, John Henry knew it was something he could not pass up. This was his opportunity to put into practice his vision for a university education that had been halted when he left Oxford. With the hope of raising money and attracting students for the new university, Newman prepared and delivered a series of lectures in Dublin on the nature and purpose of university education. These lectures would become some of the most important lectures on university education ever written, lectures which are included in textbooks and studied to this day.

Ireland already had one university, but it was a Protestant one. There were also plans for some non-denominational colleges, but there were none for the many Catholic students. They needed a Catholic school where their faith would be respected and encouraged. Fr. Newman had to consider many things when beginning this university, such as which courses should be included in the curriculum. He covered this in his lectures. For example, Newman thought that every university should have a course on natural theology; natural theology is the study of how to understand the existence of God and his attributes, or the way he is. Newman knew and realized that natural theology should be a necessary part of university studies. Without the study of God and his attributes, all the other courses would not make sense, because without God, there is nothing. If the study of God was left out, other fields of study would incorrectly take its place. This would give students a distorted view of the nature of things. Of course classes and study are what make up any university, but in addition to this, a Catholic university should offer students the sacramental life to form the soul, along with the environment for students to grow with the support and friendship of other Catholics.

Finally, Ireland's first Catholic university opened in 1854, and Fr. Newman was its first rector. He had recruited teachers from among his former students and from other respected professors. He also prepared the plans for studies and exams. Besides natural theology, courses included the classics, mathematics, literature, history, and modern languages. Newman had great vision and understanding of the needs of the modern world. He realized that faith and reason are not opposed, that scientific discoveries and theories fit well with belief in God. And so, the university soon included both a science school and a medical school.

For Newman the goal of a university is more than just preparing students to get a job or for professional careers that earn a lot of money. The goal of a university is much grander! It is "to make good men, or persons." The young people could prepare for careers in professional schools after finishing undergraduate courses, courses which would help form their intellect. Newman realized that students must learn to reason well, to recognize different concepts, to compare things, to understand the relation of individual things to the whole, and make proper judgments, that is, to reason well. These skills are necessary for a successful life in any situation. This is what Newman called 'developing a philosophical habit of mind,' that is, a certain way of thinking. If students develop this philosophical habit of mind, they are able to work afterwards in any profession, while still keeping God as number one in their hearts.

One way that Newman helped form the minds and hearts, and therefore the character, of the students was by setting up a number of collegiate houses. These houses were much more than student residences. They were places in which the students lived in a family-type setting with a head of house, a tutor, and a chaplain. In this setting, they learned from each other and helped one another while forming strong friendships.

There were other interesting ideas that Newman included in the university. In his time, during the 1800s, women did not yet attend university, but he was very forward-thinking. He allowed women to attend the classes offered in the evening. He also established a debate society which was one of the first of its kind, patterning it after a society at Oxford University. He also began a library to which his friends donated books, plus a university magazine for which he was the editor and wrote many articles.

And still, the amazing John Henry Newman did even more. He built a beautiful church for the university where students gathered on special occasions such as the opening of each year. This beautiful church is still open in Dublin today. There Fr. Newman delivered some memorable homilies. In one such homily, given on the feast of St. Monica, he compared the Catholic Church to St. Monica, the mother of St. Augustine. He told the students that the Church is like a good mother who brings her wandering children back to the faith, as St. Monica had done for her son.

The university got off to a good start. Newman was able to attract students, but sadly, it did not continue to grow. The problem was that university education was expensive, and few families could afford to send their children. Not only that, but the British government would not grant recognition to the degrees the students earned there. A bigger problem was that Archbishop Cullen, who had invited Newman to begin the university, did not understand the importance that Newman wanted to give to the laity, or people who weren't priests themselves. Newman wanted the laity to be involved in running the university, but the archbishop disagreed with this idea. So, he made Newman's work very difficult.

During this trying time, Newman expressed his frustration when he wrote to a friend, "A Rector (university president) ought to be a more showy, bustling man than I am, in order to impress the world that we are great people (. . .) I ought to dine out every day, and of course I don't dine out at all. I ought to mix in literary society and talk about new gasses and the price of labor—whereas I can't recollect what I once knew, much less get up a whole lot of new subjects." Newman realized that characteristics such as these, which he did not possess, were necessary for the success of such an institution as a university. He also said that he needed to be twenty years younger to have more strength for this demanding work. After four years as rector, in 1858, he resigned his position. Half a century later, the university became part of University College Dublin, a public university. We can learn from Newman that everyone has strengths and weaknesses, even someone with as many talents as he. Understanding one's strengths and weaknesses and acting accordingly is the virtue of prudence.

Although Newman had only succeeded in part, he had done something very important. He had inspired many teachers and students and he had shown that classical liberal arts education and forming men of character was possible and desirable. Even today, his idea of university education is honored and studied and the lectures he gave are now collected into an influential book called *The Idea of a University.*

12

Starting a Medical School

Before returning to Birmingham and leaving his position as rector of the university, Newman accomplished another important thing. He opened a medical school in Dublin. At the time there were only a few official schools for future doctors and some small private schools. Newman was concerned that there were very few Catholic professors teaching the medical students. In Dublin, 99 doctors were Protestants, and only twelve were Catholic, and out of 49 who taught medicine only two were Catholic. Newman understood that it made a difference to have Catholic teachers because a physician should keep in mind the beliefs and spiritual needs of their patients following the doctrines of the Catholic faith. For instance, he argued that some physicians did not call for a priest to care for a very sick patient reasoning that this would scare the patient by making him think he was at death's door. Another reason for educating Catholic physicians was simply to increase their number in Dublin, where they were a minority.

Despite the overwhelming majority of Catholics in the population, a Catholic medical school did not exist anywhere in Ireland because of the excessive influence which the state religion exercised over the already existing schools. Newman summed it up as follows: "The medical establishments have simply been in the hands of Protestants."

Newman discussed the need for a medical school at the Catholic University of Ireland with Andrew Ellis, a distinguished Irish doctor. Dr. Ellis had taught at a small school of medicine that was closing. With Newman's directions and the tacit approval of the bishops on the board of the university, Ellis purchased a very good building owned by his previous school. It included two large rooms, one for examining patients and the other for examining cadavers. With Ellis's advice and the recommendations of others, Newman looked for professors for the new school. He sought professors with prestige who were practicing Catholics. One of these was William Sullivan, a renowned professor of chemistry, who years later became the rector of Queen's College in Cork.

Another one was Dr. Robert Lyons who was an expert in medical pathology, especially infectious diseases. Lyons had just spent some time in an area known as Crimea, a peninsula in Eastern Europe on the Black Sea, as the chief physician with the British army, combating diseases in the war trenches. He wrote books on many subjects including forestry, and later became a member of parliament in the British Government.

Obtaining recognition for the medical degree granted by the school was very important. The professors at the school applied for formal acknowledgment by the Royal College of Surgeons in Dublin and other medical boards. Soon the students were able to be examined by these boards and have their medical degrees recognized. This ensured the success of the school.

Newman was also concerned about the overall formation of each medical student as a whole person. He wanted them to take some courses in the liberal arts and thus have a better understanding of the human person and society. He also wanted them to have a healthy environment in which to live where they would not only have their material necessities cared for, but where they could avoid the moral dangers of young men living by themselves in a large city. With this in mind, he tried to set up a medical house, or college, which would be a good lodging for the students. However, he was not in Dublin long enough to realize this goal.

The founder realized the importance of having a good place for the students to practice their skills too. He dreamed of the school having its own hospital where the environment and spiritual care would be Catholic. He asked one of the professors to try to obtain hospital privileges at Misericordia Hospital which a religious community of sisters was then starting. Alas, Newman's departure from the university did not allow him to accomplish this project.

All in all, Newman had used his leadership skills to begin a medical school that would provide a first-rate education for future doctors while teaching and supporting their religious beliefs. This would benefit many sick people and their families. It is just as important today as it was then for there to be Catholic physicians who follow the teachings of the Catholic Church. Once again, John Henry Newman was leading the way.

Almost one hundred years after Newman established a university and medical school, a different priest, Fr. Josemaría Escrivá, established the University of Navarre, another Catholic university with a medical school. Like the English educator, Fr. Escrivá was concerned with forming the minds and hearts of students, teaching them that science and faith should work in harmony. He was another great leader inspiring professors and students.

The Pen as Weapon

THE RAMBLER AND KINGSLEY AFFAIRS

There is an old saying that the pen is mightier than the sword. What does this mean? It means that many things can be accomplished with the use of words in publications. Today this is called the "media." Although the media was different in

Newman's time, in some ways, the printed word was even more powerful than today because more people read when there were no televisions, movies, or smartphones. Newman had been a writer from a young age and later an editor for different publications. These publications were influential journals which made a difference in people's way of thinking and acting. This print media, journals on history, politics, business, and religion helped shape public opinion.

An editor is a writer who organizes journals, choosing which writers and which articles should be included in a particular journal for the maximum impact. Newman had much editing experience. In Dublin he established and edited a university newspaper at the University of Ireland, and along with a professor of chemistry, he established and edited the *Atlantis*, a university journal on both literary and scientific topics.

Many of Newman's convert friends were intellectuals with knowledge and opinions in many different areas. One of these academic friends had started a journal called the *Rambler* for which Newman had written some verses. Cardinal Wiseman was behind a competing publication, the *Dublin Review*. He and others were upset with the views expressed by some of the articles in the *Rambler*. These articles, written by laymen, were on matters such as the Church's position regarding state support for Catholic schools or the temporal power of the Pope.

One particular view which caused Cardinal Wiseman to be angry was the threat to the property owned by the Pope. At that time, the Pope owned large pieces of land called papal estates; the Pope was a sort of ruler over these estates. This was considered "temporal power." Some political leaders in Italy wished to seize the Pope's lands in order to form one nation. A big controversy was raging among Catholics over whether or not the Pope should even be allowed these estates. Newman believed this to be a complicated question which could have two sides. It was at this time when an Italian army led by Garibaldi seized almost all of the papal estates, and united Italy into one country. Pope St. Pius IX had to flee for his life to the coastal city of Gaeta under Spanish protection. The Pope was able to return later to Rome, but to a much smaller area of land which is well-known today: the Vatican State.

Realizing the importance of the lay voice in these controversial matters, Newman, though he did not seek the position out, became editor of the *Rambler* to save the magazine. He thought it was important for Catholics to have a means to express their ideas in cultural, literary, and educational matters. He wanted a balanced tone in this journal which showed respect for differing opinions, something we take for granted today. Unfortunately, this was forward-thinking and Ullathorne, the Bishop of Birmingham, called Newman in and told him to step down from the magazine. This was a blow to Newman, but he obeyed his bishop. Perhaps the tone of the magazine had been argumentative and not handled well by the lay writers, but the bishops believed that laymen should simply believe and do what they were told. But Newman was ahead of his time and again acted as a brave leader. He knew that an educated laity should be allowed a voice. He thus both respected the bishops and supported the educated laity, which today is the accepted way of thinking. But Newman was not out of hot water yet and soon would have another battle which would result in one of his most famous books.

Newman turned his thoughts and efforts to the daily tasks at hand to recover from the Rambler affair. There were also more disagreements to come such as one with the London Oratory, an offshoot of the Birmingham Oratory. At this time, he was also saddened by the way he was treated by some Catholics who complained about him to the Holy See for his teaching, which they did not understand. But Newman was like a powerful lion, waiting to be roused into action. Then something happened, and this lion was awakened with a great roar, a roar which was heard by the whole of England! Who was the cause of this? It was Charles Kingsley, an Anglican priest and writer with very anti-Catholic views. Charles Kingsley did something that is hard to imagine; he accused John Henry Newman of being a liar! Not only that, he also wrote that all Catholic priests were liars! He claimed that Newman himself had said, "Truth, for its own sake, has never been a virtue with the Roman clergy. Fr. Newman informs us that it need not, and on the whole, ought not to be." Newman could not allow this kind of malicious attack against his character and against the Catholic priesthood to go unanswered.

The year was 1864. The way Newman chose to reply to Kingsley's attack was by writing a clear and reasoned argument or explanation, called an "apology." Newman's work turned into a book which explained the story of his spiritual conversion and how he had become Roman Catholic. In this Apology, Newman said that the Catholic priests he knew were simple and honest. They taught that we must speak the truth and not lie. Newman explained that although some priests gave theories of circumstances in which lying might be necessary, priests such as the respected St. Alphonse Ligouri, he, and other priests had differences of opinions on such situations. Newman observed that many Anglican teachers also noted extreme circumstances when telling a lie might be permissible. An example for this type of tricky situation would be if someone was being chased by a murderer and ran into a neighbor's house to hide. If the criminal came to that house and asked the homeowner if there was someone inside hiding, could the homeowner tell an untruth to the bad person? It all depends on different definitions of what constitutes a lie. Newman gave some very complicated and good explanations of all these things while maintaining that Christians shouldn't lie. His purpose was to defend the character of the many holy and good priests that Kingsley had defamed.

Newman wrote this now famous book, *Apologia pro vita sua*, in a very short span of a few weeks. (*Apologia* is Latin for apology). It was basically the story of his conversion to Catholicism. He wrote it by reviewing many letters he had written or received over the years. In the *Apologia* Newman explained how he came to believe in the authority of the Pope and to understand the universal nature of the Catholic Church. He had realized that Anglicans had separated themselves from the communion of the Catholic Church. The Anglican church had become a national church under the control of civil government. In this very moving spiritual autobiography, Newman showed the world through his words how hard his decision had been to leave the church he had loved, the church which felt like home. But in the Catholic Church, he found a new home, a new home in which he felt totally secure, happy, and at peace. He had realized that all that the Catholic Church taught was true.

Many people in England read the *Apologia*. This book continues to be read throughout the world and has helped many people in their decisions to convert to Catholicism. Such is the power of John Henry

Newman's words. Catholics who before had not appreciated Newman began to admire him; Anglicans who had parted ways with him rethought their opinion of him, and some renewed their correspondence and friendship with him. Indeed, one of the hardest things for Newman when leaving the Anglican church was that he lost so many friends who did not understand his conversion. This loss of friends had pained him deeply, even though he knew he was making the right choice. So, the renewal of some of these friendships was cause of great joy. One of his former students gave him a violin, a touching and thoughtful gift which made Newman very happy. The most memorable reunion was Newman's visit to his former best friends, Pusey and Keble. The men had not seen each other for such a long time that they had grown old; they almost did not recognize each other at first, yet at their meeting, their friendship was renewed.

The *Apologia* was in defense of his actions. Newman had boldly defended his character and love for truth, as well as that of Catholic priests. Once more his name became well-known throughout England, and he became a champion for English Catholics. In both the Rambler and Kingsley affairs, Newman had shown the world through his words and actions what was inside his heart.

14

Boys Are Boys

THE ORATORY SCHOOL IN BIRMINGHAM

Newman was a teacher at heart. Although the Catholic University in Dublin did not work out, he still found a way to use his talents to educate boys and young men. Some of his friends with children had asked him to start a school. Newman was interested in this project, but he told the parents, "You need to find other parents with children who wish to attend and raise money for the project." They were more than happy to comply. For his part, Newman explored a few Catholic schools in England and realizing that there were future students, he made the decision to open a school. And so it was that in 1859, just outside Birmingham, the Oratory School opened with seven boys, all sons of converts.

The purpose of the school was to provide good academics and sound Catholic teaching. In England, the existing private schools (called "public") offered good academics but did not have a good moral environment. In these schools, there was a lot of bullying, severe punishments such as flogging, and poor religious instruction.

In his school, Newman wanted the boys to be allowed to be boys. He understood that to thrive, they needed to be able to enjoy themselves and play sports, and to act with freedom without excessive control. They needed discipline without severe physical punishment, and religious formation without turning the school into a seminary where students prepare for the priesthood.

From the beginning, Newman gave importance to the parents' role in the education of their children. He wrote them often with news about their children and suggestions for their improvement. The younger children were supervised by women who acted like mothers to them. The head of these women was Mrs. Wooten, a kind and generous widow. She was a loyal support to Newman and because of this, he defended her from the headmaster who wanted to dismiss her. This headmaster wanted to take complete control of the school. As its founder, Newman had to step in and reassert his authority. Again, he had to be strong. He wrote to the headmaster, "If I wish to speak to the masters, dames (the women who cared for the boys), etc. I am not obliged to do so through you—nor need they speak to me through you." It seemed that even in the Oratory School, problems could arise!

Newman looked for good teachers who taught well and cared for the boys. One of the teachers was Gerard Manley Hopkins, another convert whom Newman had received into the Church. Hopkins was a young poet and priest who later became very famous. He is now considered one of the great English poets, and his poems are loved and studied by many still today. Newman wished the boys to learn to read and write well. But he wanted them to do more than that, he also wanted to develop their imaginations. And he knew that this meant teaching them about the Greek and Roman heroes which would both develop their imaginations and develop their abilities to write and speak well. He also wished them to read poetry and act in plays. He edited Greek plays to remove parts that were not appropriate for the boys and prepared them to put on a yearly performance. All this helped the boys to become well-rounded young men.

Naturally the religious practices were also important at the school. The boys were invited to attend Mass daily, and to pray the rosary to the Virgin Mary, but they were not compelled to do so. On special feast days they had processions and during the month of May, special devotions in honor of the Mother of God.

The students' parents wished the school to prepare their children to study later on at universities or some professional schools. Since studying at Oxford University was the hope of many students, Newman thought about how to help them keep and practice their Catholic faith there, since it was still a Protestant university.

So, in 1864 and again in 1866, encouraged by the Bishop of Birmingham, Newman tried to open a house for Catholic students at Oxford University. But most of the bishops in England opposed the idea of Catholics studying at Oxford because they thought Catholic and Protestant students should not mix. In the end the Holy See gave approval for the Birmingham Oratory to set up a mission at Oxford. However, instruction was also given that Newman should not live there because he would attract Catholic students to the university. Newman thus felt obliged to give up plans for an Oxford Mission. Upset, he told his friend Ambrose, "My monkey is up." But despite these disappointments, all of Newman's hard work bore amazing fruits. Today, the Oratory School in Birmingham and the Oratory at Oxford, which Newman had desired, continue the educational work he inspired.

15

Always Writing Letters and Books

In the time before computers and email, before cell phones and text messages, in the time even before telephones of any kind, how did friends keep in touch with each other? They could visit with one another in person, if they lived close by. But if they lived far apart, friends would have to write letters to each other. From the time he was a young boy, Newman liked to read and write. He especially liked reading literature and history and he wrote many different things in those early years including short verses. He was a boy who liked to sit and think about things. And he would write many of these thoughts and verses in letters which he would send to friends and family, especially his sisters, whom he loved.

As a college student, he bought good books that he would read and study for writing articles. He asked his friend Pusey to buy him an edition of the writings of the Church Fathers. When they arrived, he wrote his mother, "My 'Fathers' are arrived all safe—huge Fellows they are, but very cheap—one folio costs a shilling." He cherished these volumes he called "my Fathers." When he moved to Littlemore, he set up a library there. With time he bought so many books, some in different languages, that it soon become a very big library. He enjoyed the world of books because in this written world he learned about God, the world, and men from everywhere. These habits lasted throughout his long life.

Throughout his time as a priest, both Anglican and then Catholic, his vocation meant that he met and spoke with many people. When he was not meeting with people, he would immerse himself in reading and writing. He wrote many sermons, articles, and books about

God, the Bible, and religion. But he never stopped being a good friend, and he built new friendships with many men and women. And of course, this meant he wrote letters to them as well.

Although many of his books were about theology (the study of God), he also enjoyed reading novels, especially those of Sir Walter Scott like *Ivanhoe*. He also read Charles Dickens, Jane Austen, and others. He even turned his writing skills to novels and wrote two. One novel, *Callista*, is about a young fourth century woman in the North of Africa who converts from being a pagan to a Christian. The other one, as we have seen, is about a convert at Oxford.

Since he was an excellent writer who knew Latin quite well, Newman modelled his long sentences and paragraphs on those of Cicero, the renowned Roman writer. When he wrote books, it was usually because he wanted to defend Catholic teaching and respond to the mistakes of others. But his first and last books were about the Church Fathers. He published his first book when he was only 33, and his last one at the age of 80.

He was generous with his writing skills and taught others how to improve their writing. He corrected their articles, often to be included in the various journals for which he was editor. He also helped friends, including a few women, to write books. They would send him their manuscripts, and he would make suggestions. He encouraged one of his female friends to write books for children. He was also the editor of a series of books on the lives of English saints, an especially important task for Newman. For him, the saints were great teachers who inspired with their lives and writings. He recognized the need to tell their stories to the English people. When he became an Oratorian, he took St. Philip Neri, the founder of the Oratory, as his patron saint.

Newman thought that one of the best ways to know someone was to read his letters, something he knew firsthand since he himself was a letter writer. Letters are personal, and for this reason, letters give a type of written portrait of a person, giving a glimpse of what a writer thinks about and what the writer is like on the inside. It makes sense that John Henry liked saints who left a good picture of themselves through their letters. One of these was St. John Chrysostom, a fourth century saint who was the Bishop of Constantinople. St. John was banished from his diocese by the Empress Eudoxia, possibly because he sided with one of her enemies in the royal court. In addition, Chrysostom had preached against women dressing immodestly, which Empress Eudoxia interpreted as an attack against her. In letters to his friends, St. John Chrysostom describes his suffering, his faith, his love for God, and his need for friends. These inspired Newman to continue to communicate with his many friends. Newman has left to the world many volumes of his own letters, which likewise give us an intimate glance at this fascinating saint.

From Newman's many missives, we learn how he trusted in God, even as he suffered from misunderstandings, and how much he relied on the love of his friends during these difficult times. But in his letters, he also tells funny stories and teases his friends. These give insight into Newman's lighthearted side, bringing him to life as a real person. In one letter written before he became Catholic, he tells a friend about a bold convert to Catholicism who went to Littlemore to try to convert him: "I have kept my gun loaded and cocked, intending to discharge upon him, if he made a second attempt, but he has kept his peace." Of course he was teasing, so these letters show that he had a sense of humor. His letters especially show that he was sensitive and affectionate. He would sign many of them, "Affly, yrs, John Henry," short for "Affectionately Yours."

Through all his sermons, articles, verses, books, and letters, Newman had a big influence on many people, and it continues today. His body of writing was and is read and studied by lay people and by academics. His collected letters fill many volumes of books. In 1877, Trinity College at Oxford invited him to accept the position of Honorary Fellow. The president of the college wrote Newman, "I may mention that if you should do so, you will be the first person in whose case the College will have exercised the power which was given to it in 1857, and that at the present it is not contemplated to elect another Honorary Fellow." Such was the reputation Newman had at the university and in society. He replied, "accepting with a full heart an honor which is as great a surprise to me as it is a pleasure." Newman went to Oxford as the guest of the president of Trinity College and was greatly pleased by the kindness of everyone there; he had not been back for more than thirty years.

16

Newman Becomes
a Cardinal of the Church

When Newman was the rector of the Catholic University of Ireland, Cardinal Wiseman and Archbishop Cullen thought it would help the school to have him named a bishop of the Church. So Cardinal Wiseman submitted the request to Rome. Later, however, Cullen, worried that Newman would have too much power, and changed his mind. As a result, Rome did not appoint Newman as bishop. Newman had not been seeking this honor, but the request to make him a bishop was known by the public. So, when the whole thing fell through, he was, understandably, both embarrassed and saddened by the way the matter was handled, especially since nothing was explained to him.

Another bishop also treated Newman poorly, complaining to the Holy See about Newman's belief that lay people are a witness of authentic Church teaching. Nevertheless, despite being treated poorly by these two bishops, Newman was respected more and more by many other bishops. When the Church was preparing for a world meeting of bishops, Vatican Council I (1870–1871), the Pope and various bishops asked Newman to attend as an expert on theology. Newman said no, stating, "I am not a theologian." This shows us how he was thinking at the time. He did not feel appreciated in Rome, but it also shows us that he had also grown in humility.

One of the major topics in the Church at this time which was to be discussed at the Council was the question of papal infallibility, that is, whether the Pope could make mistakes when teaching. There was much confusion about this complex topic. Englishmen were worried that papal infallibility meant the Pope would rule over English citizens. Newman had to explain that this doctrine only applied to teaching about faith and morality, not about matters concerning government, science, or other such things. He further explained that conscience is the voice of God, which all must follow, even the Pope. One writer, trying to discredit papal teachings, argued that popes had not condemned crimes such as the Massacre of St. Bartholomew's Day. Newman replied, "No Pope can make evil good. No Pope has any power over those eternal moral principles which God has imprinted on our hearts and consciences."

Happily, for Newman and for the world, he was at last honored in the right way. In 1879 he was named cardinal, an honor even higher than that of bishop. Cardinals are the highest-ranking priests in the Church. They advise the Pope, and they meet in Rome to elect a new pope after a pope dies. It was Pope Leo XIII who chose to make Newman a cardinal. This was one of his first official acts after he was elected. When someone asked Leo XIII, "What is the program (what plans do you have?) for your pontificate?" he replied, "Look who I will make my first cardinal." This meant that he admired Newman and Newman's writing. Pope Leo XIII wanted to show that Newman's teachings on the Church's doctrines were very good, and he also wanted to honor the English people by choosing one of their own to become a cardinal.

But even this deserved honor did not come automatically to the highly respected and now elderly John Henry Newman. A second time he was almost prevented from being recognized by the Church. This time it was Cardinal Edward Manning, the archbishop of Westminster, who tried to stop the appointment. Cardinal Manning was jealous of Newman, so he planned to tell Rome that Newman was not interested in becoming a cardinal. Luckily, his mean plan became known and the Duke of Norfolk and others asked for Newman's appointment. Pope Leo XIII told an English Lord, "My Cardinal! It was not easy; it was not easy. They said he was too liberal, but I had determined to honor the Church in honoring Newman (. . .) I am proud I was able to honor such a man."

And so it was that in March of 1879, Newman travelled to Rome to receive the red hat from the Pope. The red color of the hat is a symbol that a cardinal is willing to die to defend the Pope. Leo XIII welcomed Newman with great affection. However, not long before meeting the Pope, two of Newman's friends had died, Ambrose St. John and Edward Caswall. The thought of losing his two beloved friends caused him to cry. When he told the Pope about his friends' deaths, he shed some tears. The Pope placed his hand on Newman's head and kindly said, "Don't cry." Newman's ability to feel so deeply for his friends shows us how much he loved and that, in the right circumstance, leaders can cry too.

A day earlier, before this moving encounter with Pope Leo XIII, Newman gave a speech in Rome against liberalism in religion. This speech both summed up the teaching of his life and defended the Church. Newman said that liberalism in religion is "the doctrine that there is no positive truth in religion, that one creed is as good as another." Some people then, like today, embraced the mistaken teaching that all religions are the same, that no one religion is true or better. Newman proclaimed that such liberal ideas hold that "revealed religion is not a truth, but a sentiment and a taste . . ." Newman was teaching against the notion that we pick and choose a religion the way we might choose between one flavor of ice cream and another. Newman, as always, was brave in preaching and teaching the truths of the Catholic Church.

After this momentous trip to Rome, Newman, old and tired but happy, returned from Rome to England with much fanfare. Everyone, Protestants and Catholics alike, wanted to greet him and congratulate him. Four friends, including one who had been his assistant at the Littlemore church, presented him with the gift of a carriage. Newman felt that at long last, the Holy See had recognized that what he taught was correct. The peoples' kindness made him so very happy. He appreciated it greatly. But even in the joy of this honor and homecoming, sadness came into Newman's life. His sister, Jemima, died on Christmas Day of the same year, at the age of seventy-two.

17

Ready for Heaven

HIS LAST MASS, 1890

n the year 1880, John Henry Newman turned 79 years old. His life had been one of many varied experiences; he had lived through adventures, through new beginnings, through false starts, through hardships, and also many successes. He had made many friends. And he had lost many, too. Most had already died. His years were catching up with him and his health was poor. Even something mild, like a cold, would make him ill for a long time. At the beginning of the year, he fell in his room and broke a rib. A broken rib makes breathing, talking, walking, and sleeping very painful. One month later, he fell again and broke two more ribs. But even with these setbacks, when he felt well enough, he continued receiving visitors. With the help of a good friend who was a priest, he could also still reply to letters.

Though he was elderly, he continued his studying, writing, and preaching. He worked hard on preparing and publishing a revised translation of some of the writings of another one of his favorite Church Fathers, St. Athanasius, Bishop of Alexandria, in Egypt. St. Athanasius was one of the most important early Fathers who helped explain and defend the doctrine of Jesus Christ as God at the Council of Nicea. Newman admired this champion of the Faith. So even as Newman was becoming older and feebler, he was making his life count, working for God.

That same year Newman visited the Duke of Norfolk in London and preached at St. Aloysius Church in Oxford. One friend who saw Newman told his daughter, Anne Pollen, about his visit with Newman. Anne reported that when Newman complained of his health, saying that he was 79, her father, replied, "My dear Cardinal, do you forget that Blücher won the Battle of Waterloo at 85?" The cardinal replied with a smile, "Yes, and Radetsky was 92." Newman still had his memory and good sense of humor.

In the nineteenth century, Newman's time, and earlier, only famous or wealthy people had portraits of themselves made. Newman was fortunate to be both painted and photographed. This is very nice for us today, too, because we know what he looks like. Some years earlier, various artists had painted John Henry Newman, since he was so well-known. In 1881, when he went to preach at the London Oratory, he sat for the established painter, John Millais. The result was the now celebrated portrait of Newman wearing the red cape and red beretta on his head, the garments worn by cardinals. Anne Pollen went to see the painting and reported, "It is magnificent; it gives the dignity, gentleness and strength of his face, a most powerful portrait." And the artist's daughter commented that the cardinal is a "beautiful old man." He certainly was. His face, though aged, shows the gentle eyes of a saint to be.

As the months passed, Newman's strength and health weakened. His eyesight worsened, and he began to fall often. He could no longer write at all, but had to dictate his letters for others. Writing letters was still very important to him, though now his letters were short, unlike the long letters he was accustomed to. He had to decline many invitations, even from important people. However, he still managed to travel to Oxford to visit an old student, now dying, who had been a non-believer. Fr. Newman, as long as he was able, was still trying to win souls for Christ.

Though his body was failing, the cardinal maintained his mental faculties and was intellectually active. And he was still publishing! He wrote and published an important article on the inspiration of the Bible. He was consulted by people including Prime Minister Gladstone. When the former Bishop of Birmingham, then retired, visited Newman, out of humility, Newman knelt for a blessing. The bishop wrote, "I felt annihilated in his presence, there is a saint in that man!"

Until the very end of his life, Cardinal Newman showed his concern and charity towards others. Only a few months before his death, he heard that some Catholic girls working at a nearby factory run by Quakers were obliged to attend a daily Quaker religious instruction. On a cold November day with snow on the ground, he rode to the factory and walked to see the management. He spoke to them on behalf of the rights of the girls' conscience to say their own prayers; he won over the management. Upon getting back into the carriage, Newman said, "If I can but do work such as that, I am happy and content to live on." A few days later he was given the news that a room in the factory was set apart for the Catholic girls to say their own prayers.

In December 1890, Newman celebrated his last Mass; it was on Christmas Day. How he had loved the Mass! He knew God came to the altar at every Mass. As much as he wanted to, he had become too weak to celebrate the Holy Sacrifice daily. He knew his end was near, that he would soon see his Maker and Savior. He was nearing judgment before God, and by the mercy of God, one day, heaven. All his life he had believed and taught what the Bible says, that a Christian must be conscious of, and strive for, heaven; a Christian must daily prepare for heaven, for holiness is necessary to see God.

Newman realized that no one is ever fully ready for heaven. In his longest and most famous poem "The Dream of Gerontius" Newman imaginatively described the personal judgment before the Merciful Judge of a dying man at the moment of death. In the poem, Newman described how the sight of God will burn while it transforms. The man asks his guardian angel to take him away to purgatory.

When we die, we can't know how we will do before Jesus, our Savior and Judge. If we desire to be with God in heaven, we must keep his commandments daily and try to have a pure heart. We must try to remain in a state of grace by receiving the sacraments regularly. But if anyone was ready for heaven, it was John Henry Newman.

And so it was that on August 9th, 1891, Newman walked into his room, tired, but standing upright. His secretary said that he had a look of cheerfulness and thankfulness, and he spoke some kind words. It was as if he knew he was going to die. During the night he developed a serious lung infection. The next day he lay in bed very ill and was given the anointing of the sick in preparation for death. On the 11th of August, he was unconscious most of the day. He breathed his last that evening shortly before nine o'clock.

It is no surprise that the conscientious and well-organized Newman had given instructions for his burial. It took place a week later in Birmingham, and he was buried in the same grave with his best friend, Fr. Ambrose St. John. Burial in the same grave was not uncommon in the Victorian age. The pall covering the casket had his motto: *Cor ad cor loquitur* (heart speaks to heart). These words, which Newman himself had chosen, were inspired by St. Francis de Sales. This motto emphasizes the importance that Newman gave to friendship. Newman had spent his life building and nurturing friendships, through personal encounters and through all his many letters. He knew that in friendship we speak best by our hearts, through love. His simple tombstone had the inscription *Ex umbris et imaginibus in veritatem* (from shadows and images into truth). These beautiful words summed up his life; he had gone gradually from the shadows of doubts and mistakes to the truth of the Faith.

After his death, many other popes have shown their admiration and love for Newman and his writings. St.

Pius X wrote a letter to an Irish bishop explaining that John Henry Newman's teaching was reliable. Years later, St. John Paul II declared Newman to be venerable, the first step in the Church's official recognition of someone's holiness. After more study of his life and the miraculous cure of a judge, Pope Benedict XVI declared Newman blessed, and traveled to Birmingham, England to beatify him on September 19, 2010. The judge had a very serious back condition that caused much pain and made him unable to walk. After asking Newman's prayers, he was able to get up from his hospital bed and walk without pain.

Some years later a wife and mother had a life-threatening condition during her pregnancy. One day she was bleeding from the womb and she cried out to Blessed Newman for his help. The bleeding stopped immediately and she noticed the scent of roses surrounding her (a sign sometimes associated with miracles). Some months later she had a healthy baby. After recognizing this cure as miraculous, Pope Francis decided to canonize Newman. On October 13, 2019, he was declared a saint of the Catholic Church at St. Peter's Square in Rome, along with four women.

Newman had once replied to a grandnephew who asked him, "Which is greater a cardinal or a saint?" Newman replied, "Cardinals belong to this world, and saints to heaven." He did not think he was a saint. I think we know the answer as it applies to Newman: a saint is greater. Saints are normal men and women who fight day in and day out to live as children of God, to do what God asks of them. With the examples of saints like John Henry Newman, and with God's help, you too can be a saint. Perhaps some of the following prayers from this saint that follow can help you pray as he did.

• • •

18

Verses and Prayers
of St. John Henry Newman

The following are a few of the many wonderful passages from meditations and verses Newman composed. He wrote in elegant nineteenth century English. It takes a while to get used to this style, and it might take some time to follow, but soon after we can appreciate its beauty.

Each Person's Mission in Life

God has created me to do Him some definite service. He has committed some work to me which He has not committed to another. I have my mission. I may never know it in this life, but I shall be told it in the next. I am a link in a chain, a bond of connection between persons. He has not created me for naught. I shall do good; I shall do His work. I shall be an angel of peace, a preacher of truth in my own place, while not intending it if I do but keep His commandments.

Therefore, I will trust Him, whatever I am, I can never be thrown away. If I am in sickness, my sickness may serve Him, in perplexity, my perplexity may serve Him. If I am in sorrow, my sorrow may serve Him. He does nothing in vain. He knows what He is about. He may take away my friends. He may throw me among strangers. He may make me feel desolate, make my spirits sink, hide my future from me. Still, He knows what He is about.

Poem "Lead Kindly Light"—Prayer of trust in God's Providence

LEAD, Kindly Light, amid the encircling gloom
Lead Thou me on!
The night is dark, and I am far from home—
Lead Thou me on!
Keep Thou my feet; I do not ask to see
The distant scene—one step enough for me.

I was not ever thus, nor pray'd that Thou
Shouldst lead me on.
I loved to choose and see my path, but now
Lead Thou me on!
I loved the garish day, and, spite of fears,
Pride ruled my will: remember not past years.

So long Thy power hath blest me, sure it still
Will lead me on,

O'er moor and fen, o'er crag and torrent, till
The night is gone;
And with the morn those angel faces smile
Which I have loved long since, and lost awhile.

Act of Love for God

. . . And therefore, O my dear Lord, since I perceive Thee to be so beautiful, I love Thee, and desire to love Thee more and more. Since Thou art the One Goodness, Beautifulness, Gloriousness, in the whole world of being, and there is nothing like Thee, but Thou art infinitely more glorious and good than even the most beautiful of creatures, therefore I love Thee with a singular love, a one, only, sovereign love. Everything, O my Lord, shall be dull and dim to me, after looking at Thee. There is nothing on earth, not even what is most naturally dear to me, that I can love in comparison of Thee. And I would lose everything whatever rather than lose Thee. For Thou, O my Lord, art my supreme and only Lord and love.

Prayer to Jesus, Light of the Soul

Stay with me, and then I shall begin to shine as Thou shinest: so to shine as to be a light to others. The light, O Jesus, will be all from Thee. None of it will be mine. No merit to me. It will be Thou who shinest through me upon others.

Prayer to Jesus in the Holy Eucharist

I come to Thee, O Lord, not only because I am unhappy without Thee, not only because I feel I need Thee, but because Thy grace draws me on to seek Thee for Thy own sake, because Thou art so glorious and beautiful. I come in great fear, but in greater love. O may I never lose, as years pass away, and the heart shuts up, and all things are a burden, let me never lose this youthful, eager, elastic love of Thee. Make Thy grace supply the failure of nature. Do the more for me, the less I can do for myself. The more I refuse to open my heart to Thee, so much the fuller and stronger be Thy supernatural visitings, and the more urgent and efficacious Thy presence in me.

The Holy Family

When, for our sakes, the Son came on earth and took our flesh, yet He would not live without the sympathy of others. For thirty years He lived with Mary and Joseph and thus formed a shadow of the Heavenly Trinity on earth. O the perfection of that sympathy which existed between the three! Not a look of one, but the other two understood, as expressed, better than if expressed in a thousand words—nay more than understood, accepted, echoed, corroborated. It was like three instruments absolutely in tune which all vibrate when one vibrates, and vibrate either one and the same note, or in perfect harmony.

The first weakening of that unison was when Joseph died. It was no jar in the sound, for to the last moment of his life, he was one with them, and the sympathy between the three only became more intense, and more sweet, while it was brought into new circumstances and had a wider range in the months of his declining, his sickness, and death. Then it was like an air ranging through a number of notes performed perfectly and exactly in time and tune by all three. But it ended in a lower note than before, and when Joseph went, a weaker one. Not that Joseph, though so saintly, added much in volume of sound to the other two, but sympathy, by its very meaning, implies number, and, on his death, one, out of three harps, was unstrung and silent.

Praise to the Holiest (Dream of Gerontius)

Praise to the Holiest in the height
And in the depth be praise:
In all His words most wonderful;
Most sure in all His ways!

O loving wisdom of our God!
When all was sin and shame,
A second Adam to the fight
And to the rescue came.

O wisest love! that flesh and blood
Which did in Adam fail,

Should strive afresh against the foe,
Should strive and should prevail;

And that a higher gift than grace
Should flesh and blood refine,
God's Presence and His very Self,
And Essence all-divine.

O generous love! that He who smote
In man for man the foe,
The double agony in man
For man should undergo;

And in the garden secretly,
And on the cross on high,
Should teach His brethren and inspire
To suffer and to die.

Acknowledgments

I wish to express my gratitude to Barb Wyman who helped me to write this book, and to Robert Singerline for his interest and support. I also wish to thank Manix Abrera for his beautiful artwork, and Meredith Koopman for the final editing. Lastly I wish to gratefully acknowledge the importance for me of St. Josemaría Escrivá, founder of Opus Dei, and his teaching on Christian holiness.